Reality:
Truth,
Words
and Love

Reality:
Truth, Words and Love

Vincent M. Riccardi

To order additional copies of this book, contact:
Xlibris
844-714-8691
www.Xlibris.com
Orders@Xlibris.com
845345

CONTENTS

To Susan Leona Bogda Riccardi, the basis for our reality.
I started writing the poems in medical school to give voice
to feelings in contrast to the hard-fact science characterizing
the curriculum. The poetry was emphasized when I met my
wife, Susan. I continued through to present, being convinced
as a genetic scientist-clinician that the most important reality
had its origin in relationships between two people.
Sue and I have realized that reality for fifty-five years as of 2022!

Preface

The mélange of poetry shared here develops internal connections respecting the elements of its title and the lifelong sensibilities of the author. The title of the collection revolves around how we, as modern people, realize *reality* as a function of *truth* as revealed through the innuendo of *words* and the existentialism of *love*—Reality, truth, words, love. These elements are manifest in the most mundane and commonplace facts and phenomena through to the most arcane and erudite ideas and emotions. We usually separate erudite and mundane, on the one hand, and facts and emotions, on the other. But here is an effort to mix the two extremes with each other and the in between. Not included in the title is something embedded—some might say "implicit"—in the four words just discussed: time. That is, reality, truth, words, and love all require (or, in some way, depend on) time for their respective intensions and extensions (as Ludwig Wittgenstein might say). Time is an element of reality, and that fact is in the many of the poems shared here. The reader should be sensitive both to the unspoken allusions to time and the spoken ones (e.g., *moments*, *first*, etc.). Juxtaposing these elements and the circumstances of their manifestations hopefully provides a new perspective on the life that is the reality for us in the twenty-first century.

Acknowledgments

Thanks to my wife, Susan Leona Riccardi, and Marie-Paul Mussche, Steven D. Rhodes, Tibby Lee, John Kralik, and Leslie Holmes for their encouragement and feedback!

Again and Again

An instance
of coincidence
more than once
has become a moment
mutually transcendent,
as tho' you and I are sent
to each other to begin
again and again
that final necessity,
an alternative reality.

And you know where
reality begins: Here
in the midst of what
we want to put first
because it makes sense
at the time and awakens
our otherwise dormant,
torpid lives in testament
to the passions that we are.

All of Us

When someone invokes "pandemic," it means
all of us! Every single person—deans
and students, Presidents and the voters,
the recipients and the promoters;
I, with my sought-after medical degree,
and they who expect I'll share it for free.
The clowns and those they bring to laughter.
Those who come before or who trail after.
We are all susceptible and may die
whether we seem to be lowly or high—
as we hope for no procrastination
in developing a vaccination!

Alone in a Spring Rain

How wet my skin
with Spring rain.
Yet, deep inside
my soul has dried,
like an aged grape
whose wrinkled shape
belies the wine
that might have been.
Luscious fruit of Dionysus,
miscegenous humor and pulp,
the promise of noble nectar
lost to desiccation.

Arrivederci, Joe Zisa

Joe, for years, we shared
Saturday and Sunday afternoons
at Up th' Hill—solving the
world's problems and becoming
special friends, or "goombas," as
Sinatra would have sung it. And you
did the impossible: you made me
a better pool player. And even
more than that, you became part
of my life, no less part of my family
than my grandkids, who knew you were
"King of th' Hill," crowned every May 27.
Word has it that I am a better man
because of you—a fact declared
every time I put the 8-ball where
it belongs. You put me where
I belong. Love, Doc.

ATPome ATPoem

The work of being alive,
the push, the pressure, the drive,
is accounted for by letters three—
the flameless burn of ATP.

Aurora's Gold Canary Blues

Coal mines made my daddy black with slurry.
He said my songs were the cure for my pain.
His baby girl, a sunshine-singing gold canary.

My friends they tell me to be merry.
They don't know how bad's the pain.
I'm just their smiling, pretty gold canary.

My doctor tells me not to worry.
But he don't know my awful pain.
To him I'm just a patient gold canary.

I think of how coal miners scurry
when they see the death with no pain
of the breathless tell-tale gold canary.

My health plan tells me not to worry.
But they don't know my awful pain.
To them I'm just a costly gold canary.

They send me down their mine in a hurry
to test a system to avoid money pain,
a dollar-saving, experimental gold canary.

I don't want to be in no cemetery.
But I know my loss is their gain
as I become an angel, once a gold canary.

Banning High School Reunion

Michael Nott, Bob Waldron, Vic Riccardi
were always punctual, never tardy
at Carson Elementary, where Mrs. Strong
taught second grade and helped us to belong
to each other as very special friends.
But the outcome of that magic still depends
on what happened later in other schools.
As Wilmington Warriors we were nobody's fools,
sharing times good, times bad, preparing us
to be Banning Pilots, even daring us
to grow up, to make decisions about college
and beyond, to employ special knowledge
for the good of others. In Nineteen Fifty-Eight
after graduation, decisions and fate
sent us on separate paths seemingly diverse.
But here tonight we see it's actually the reverse.
We simply took different roads and used something true
we got to know at Banning—whatever you do
make it count for something special beyond
yourself. This commitment to others is the bond
that makes us all proud of Banning as teacher.
So say we three, the Doctor, Judge and Preacher.

Baptismal Eucrasy

The blue, cold rushing
forest stream floods
her brow and breasts
in tender bold rushing,
in reiterating fantasy, like
a seething dream, as he
floods her with white heat,
transforming the moment
into sublime communion.

Bereft of Friendship

I have friends.
Quite a few, I think.

Episodic sharing that dwindles—
      without summation
      or derivatives;
      calculus with canceling variables.

Love is alternative to friendship—
women are exclusive about which.

I am lonely thereby.

Friendship excluded by love—
      sexual or mystical.
I am lonely.
      Very lonely.

Blue Diamond Blues

Kissin' my baby in the backseat o' my car.
My blue diamonds are home, locked in a jar.
I got the blue diamond blues.

My baby is ready for all that I got.
Does she know blue diamonds make me so hot?
I got the blue diamond blues.

I try so hard to rise to th' occasion,
but I need blue diamond's friendly persuasion.
I got the blue diamond blues.

What I need now is firm resolution.
I look to my baby for this problem's solution.
I got the blue diamond blues.

She reaches inside her blue diamond mine.
Handing me one, she says "Hon, you'll do fine."
I had the blue diamond blues.

In just a few minutes I's ready for action,
givin' my baby some deep satisfaction.
I ain't got no blue diamond blues.

Body and Mouth as a Voice

The first time I saw Amber Lynn
was in the movie, "The Devil in Miss Jones,"
naked, engaged and limber in
sex with two men, perfunctory moans
accenting the visual image placing
her in a distinctive social realm,
presumably never to be gracing
a fund-raising program to overwhelm
and beat back some awesome disease.
Yet, there she was on birthday twenty-eight
as public fund-raiser, gracious and at ease,
displaying a warm, compassionate state,
arousing concern for others I'd not expected.
Among the crowd of porn stars were two infants
whose mothers were acknowledged and respected
both for these babes and for the many instants
they'd shared themselves; naughty for a price.
Happy, then and now: sincere and candid smiles.
No twisted, forlorn grimaces implying a slice
of flesh painfully exacted while making miles
of film. In truth they actively pursued
a satisfaction based on their own wants:
plain old enjoyment, not being subdued.
Amber and her friends have countered the taunts
poisoning so many people's minds about
what is natural, pleasant and fulfilling.
Their demeanors and countenance leave no doubt
but that women of their ilk are willing
merely to be public about what all
women would want at least to consider:

sex lives with choice, more like a shopping mall
than a backroom store; not some bitter
acquiescence to a single venue, to stare
at the ceiling for two to three moments
while some man is driven to snare,
to capture. I am inclined to proponents
of pornography as a quiet, liberating
force, ultimately giving realistic choice
to women thoughtful and discriminating:
Both mouth and body finally have a voice.

Buss to the Future

Our dinners that night included
rattlesnake roasted with pumpkin seeds
and salmon white from an octopus diet.
We engaged so sweetly;
smart elegance and cautious intelligence.
Dialogue about sensibilities
in the context of existential prose
and respect for the poetry
of where reality begins.
The dénouement, my final gesture,
a heartfelt handshake
that became a clumsy embrace,
cheek to cheek.
Then, unexpectedly, your kiss,
a buss on my lips, lingering yet.
Concupiscence or camaraderie?
Concerns for the future
that may never be
as the realities of ambivalence
or presumed compromise
supervene?

Café au Lait Spots

The skin is quite deep.
It must hide and reveal.
Niimura Sensei knows.

Small lumps and brown spots
brought us together to turn
chaos into truth.

My friend understands jokes.
He knows my life is a joke.
We laugh together.

Captive

For a moment, I'm finally free, alone. Yet,
part of me expects your intrusion into my reverie,
displacing the pleasure and peace of my solitude.
I listen to old songs and read a new book.
Then, as if by magic, a fragment of the music—
not otherwise important—revives your presence.
We are one again as I close my book.

Captured Moments

Mother sprawled on the floor,
anger thick in the air:
primordial sense of causation;
omnipotent, trembling in my crib.

And later, when you were her
age, tenderness mixed with
hilarious laughter of turmoil
on our honeymoon night—
a rice kernel hidden by foreskin.
I wish I could have laughed too.

You're almost gone, but not quite.
I still have your kiss
captured, somehow mingled with
the sprawling and crib power
I'd known long before.
I still feel the soft, sweet
fullness of your breasts
in all the ways we shared them.
Your sweetness. And your reticence
that only now I understand
was your terror about being
sprawled by the blows,
the ugliness you'd captured
elsewhere on your own, but
could not displace from me.

Choreography

I want to dance with you.
to renew a pact
perhaps never begun.
I want to share with you
what may not stand well as fact
but is none the less
the final beginning
of my reality,
the incredible substance
at the center of everything
I am or hope to be.
But to share we must dance,
move in unison, in concert,
two perspectives, two centers
melded by the rhythm
and the common effort
to reach new centers
arising in the movement and form
of our dancing.
The terpsichore of the moment
is the nidus of our sharing,
that vague fact spent
as a declaration of love.

Claire Leonard

Just out of the wheelchair, now in my first
faculty position, I was ready to burst
on the genetics scene, knowing I could not dare
without a fellow to spark me: her name was Claire.
She was youthful, dedicated, smart 'n'
ready to go, already published with Barton.
So, we concocted a plan to do genetic stuff
in both Denver so genteel and the rough
outbacks of Colorado and Wyoming,
plus Nebraska and Salt Lake City, roaming
at least once a week. Thus, we traveled a lot,
but the care that we gave and the learning we got
made it good. Then, she went her separate way.
She assumed new work as I began to play.
Eventually, the city known by its lake
became her grounds. She would smartly take
the stuff of Ray White and of Carey
and of others, finally to marry
the heart and the soul of clinical care
in her name: my colleague, my friend, Claire.

Code Blue Blues

They say when you suddenly fall on your back
and you seem to be having a bad heart attack,
they call a "code blue" and start in to use
what gets you a-singin' the code blue blues.

I'm down on the floor, feeling like dead,
the drugs and the pain swirlin' 'round in my head.
I hope they keep on treatin'! Oh, please don't refuse!
So, I keep repeatin' these code blue blues.

A nurse keeps pushin' down on my chest,
another calls a priest to see that I'm blessed.
The shocks and the pushin' burn and contuse.
Oh, please keep me singin' the code blue blues.

I don't want to die, I's just startin' to groove!
Oh, Lord, let my health plan quickly approve.
Don't tell me their promos were just phony ruse,
with a limit on singin' the ol' code blue blues.

Well, they paid after fussing and initial resisting,
then canceled renewal for attacks preexisting!
I just can't get away from terrible news
since I started singin' the code blue blues.

Colorado

When I saw you last, the Colorado
was swollen, raging bravado
hurrying to meet the Gulf and mix
Texas silt with a gentler wave that licks

and tickles the shore. Now the seething, bone
blistering sun, abandoned and alone
in azure sky marks the time and reflects
my own state. Your absence has affects

neither of us would have guessed
weeks (or was it years) ago when you pressed
your fingers on my skin and your heart
on my soul, melting and fusing part

of me into who you are and what we
might be when the river and the sea
again become the focus of life within
a life. But until we can begin—

anew, again or never—what heaven's kiss
holds as promise, please know that I miss
you.

Complete

Part of me doesn't work.
In this sense, I'm incomplete.
But that's who I am.
And I like who I am.

I don't like being without
the completeness of myself.
But that's who I am.
And I like who I am.

We cannot be joined.
In this sense, I'm incomplete.
But that's who I am.
And I like who I am.

I don't like being without
the completeness of you.

Complicity

I once suggested to a woman
I'd loved that we actually had
been complicit in life.
She said: "More."
We did.

I once suggested to a woman
I'd loved that we actually had
been complicit in life.
She said: "What?"
We died.

Compulsion Clouded

Oh, life unjoy
I could not go
but as the arrow
told me so.
"To the left:"
thus, I cleft.
"To the right:"
with all my might.
Now, as the arrow points,
my soul disjoints
as I would go
not as the arrow
tells me so.

You are unjoy
as now one joy,
a vintage wine,
a flower of nine
petals,
settles
with sweet inflection
to cloud direction.

Joy must be joint
and does not point,
but just allows
for any "nows"
to be favored
and savored
forever.

Never
such joy
since I've grown
have I known
'til this
quiet bliss.

Consequences

We spend so much time doing what
accounts for the results later. But
the huge interim efforts are a null
compared to the functions that pull
beginning or endpoint front and center—
as though there's no way to enter
reality except for selective inclusion
of only the start and conclusion:
the in-between progressive pale shades
are lost as the brightest light simply fades.

Couplets 2002–2013

These ditties begin with our sweet Texas Amy.
We know that her "Fa" will come after "Do-Re-Mi."

There is a kid whose name is Andy.
His looking at ladies is very randy.

There is a girl whose name is Angela.
She likes fruit, especially banangela.

There is a woman whom we call Bonita.
In this big ol' world there's no one sweeta.

There is a guy whose name is Chris.
He's the one our Urs and the fish will kiss.

There is a woman that we all call Donna.
She chews things up like a hungry piranha.

Rhyming is tough for sweet cousin Emily.
So, skip the metaphor and resort to simile.

There is a guy whose name is Ernie.
His time on earth's been a naughty journey.

There is a girl whose name is Ginny.
She's got an in-law who should be "Vinnie."

There is a cutie we all call Hop.
Dancing and singing she'll never stop.

We have a cat whose name is Hugo.
He's always asking: "Where did Sue go?"

There is a girl we call Kylee Kay.
Our girlie-girl beams in her smiley way.

There is a girl whose name is Mikah.
She rides around on her motor bikah.

And right next to her is cute cousin Mike.
And he's been that way since he was a tyke.

There is a kid whose name is Nick.
Cars he'll crash and his nose he'll pick.

And Sue's brother Pete is quick to quip:
make out the check not to "Pete" but "Bip."

There is a guy whose name is Rich.
He knows the diff. 'tween rhythm and pitch.

There is a guy whose name is Ryan,
who no one here has ever seen cryin'.

There is a girl whose name is Sue.
Many are here 'cause she likes to . . .

There is a girl whose name is Ursula.
When she drives, we call her Cursula.

There is a guy whose name is Vic.
He can treat you when you're sick.

Cross

I am more than me:
the sky, the woods, the tree
shaped into a simple cross
to remind us of a loss
that is really where I begin,
His death discounting sin.

Cups for Wine

The cup of my
memory,
filled to its brim
with the wine
that's yours and mine,
at times o'erflows
and I long to cup
my lips to yours
to share this nectar
so sweet, so alive.

Dad (Ralph)

For a long time, my dad's life
involved applying heat to
to two metal surfaces that become one.
He could always barter this skill
to enhance our resources.
I sometimes wondered what it'd have
been like for us to be so welded,
melded, joined as two men,
adding to the formula of father and son.
I knew him as my dad,
almost never as a man—a person
with compelling needs and expectations.
He was my father, I the son—
a special son—the oldest son of the
oldest son for eight generations.
We were never two men together.
Yet, he was always there and
always proud of himself, of me.
And now that I am in the middle of
my eighth decade—where he was
when the Alzheimer's unraveled
him and he was beyond sharing—
I begin to know what we missed.
But I was involved elsewhere.

I think I missed something.
I am vaguely aware of what he
probably wanted, but unselfishly

never demanded or imposed.
I miss him. And I miss his
not being the father to my son.
That I had no son is in
many ways beside the point.
I need to be able to share something
that seems to require paternity,
even if it's indirect.

My legacy seems incomplete—
both for what Ralph and I let slip by then
and for what is slipping by now:
to blossom, to regale without the logic,
but simply a reflection of
our same Y-chromosome.
Can another Y participate? Yes.
but the distractions are compounded thereby, therein.
Does it make sense to pursue these matters?
Is this about neurosis or about something
more wholesomely biological?
Am I trying to obviate or abrogate being a twit?
Or have I come to realize a biological truth—
a bit too late, as it were?
In this digital era, when information,
facts and virtual feelings are ubiquitous,
supplanting "wisdom," I want to be
wise to my son, with my son.
This is not a compromise of my three
daughters any more than their
gravidity is a compromise:
simply a fact about when and how
two generations engage.

The portending of father and son
is surely missed.
Yet, this is not solely a lament.
Rather, I mean to encourage my juniors
not to wait too long, not to miss the
uniquely satisfying glory of knowing—
and being known to—your father.

Declarations of Rain

Sun-shower in Hong Kong harbor
rekindles the glow of other
rains and other ports.
What did we have in those
other places in other times
that eludes me now?
Your face and breasts
against my own,
my heart was pounding,
our souls a single vortex.
Your face and breasts
distant impressions that
force the issue still,
but cannot declare it.
My soul languid, at rest,
a literal reality at best;
where is the poetry,
the rhymes that were
our declaration?
The declaring,
the declaration,
the declared?

Words can neither disguise
nor reify what we have been
and they do not share
how much I miss you.

Denouement

I am what I know of
of myself and many others.

I am what was that is
now confined to my brain.

When my brain no longer
breaches the confines, I am not:

I become merely the knowledge
of others and, oh, so briefly.

Determination

My trajectory, is really a life
that goes on and on and on so that strife
essentially plays no part in the "Yes"
or "No" choice that could be made, nor a "Guess"
that often determines whether I proceed.
It is as though there is some urgent need
that's part of a "Guess," but is otherwise left
to the unknown, a wild surge bereft
of truth. The truth does not count at all:
"Stay alive at any price" is the Call!

Dusk in Germany

A lingering and sometimes rainy dusk
accentuates the nostalgic rust,
the romantic risk in castles and foothills
along the Rhine. The peaceful order stills

to a whisper my excited calling out
of your name in the fitful turnabout
that has marked my dreams since the start.
In the instant of your turn, I see part

of your face, wet and whimsical, which may
reflect a thousand different truths to play
on as my calls to you resound and echo
in my reverie and the regimented glow

along the river's edge removes my voice
from your name. I no longer have a choice,
I know, about what you or we might
have been, as dusk gives way to night.

Early-Morning Neighbors

The resounding ring of the circular saw
cuts through the air, slicing one thought from
the next. Otherwise, the neighborhood is
quiet, the main sound the running water
next door. Visually, the finches finish
the supply of seeds we'd left. They push
one another from the feeder according
to rules I can't fathom. Maybe there
are none. More likely, just subtle. But, back
to the backyard. Now a hammer pounds on
wood. What're they building? It's my
right to write the details. I am one of
three adjacent neighbors. Their sounds are
my sounds: for completeness.

Echoes of August

The sweltering of Virginia's summer heat
unexpectedly intensified by the wild beat
of hearts in trembling unison,
an endless moment, two in one.

Ecstasy

Sometimes the past and what comes next
join in the present in such a way that the text

describing the interdigitation conspicuously misses
the point. It is not about then, the kisses

spilt on vacant mouths. It is not about later,
the kisses traveled on some nascent incubator.

You and I are now, not then, not later. We are
the matter, the stuff of now, the center, the star

at the origin. I am enchanted by the way you show
me who you are, the way you speed up or slow

down. You are not everything. You are one of those toys
that sets limits: the place between girls and boys

that really makes a difference between the lines
of women and men and how the effort sublimely mines

love from the effort. How hard do I strive
as opposed to what is the reward of where I arrive?

I want to walk into it, walk into the ecstasy. There you are.

Empty Ballot

The moon is full but the skies are clouded,
and my mind is racing, overcrowded
with images and words from two disparate
sources who vainly, shamefully parrot
words that once were true, but now simply rhyme.
They're but a silly song, an empty mime.
Where is the truth that helps us remember
the warm summer sun in bleak November
when we cast our votes? Alas, we resort
merely to vague passions that barely support
worried election of a President
who poses a risk without precedent.

Expectant Thanks

You have been gone for so long
that only I know what's wrong

is a result of your not being here
as I engage the future with a blank stare

or while I settle on the invigorating
softness of a woman whose pulsating

movements remind me of the collusion
our own bodies contributed to the illusion

that we were everything, all that life
was or could be, the present rife

with the future, pregnant expectations
transforming or obscuring situations

that otherwise might merely be the bland,
sterile encounters that surreptitiously stand

in for reality. I am impoverished
by your absence, the properly relinquished

claim on the present, the sweetly fecund
community that must needs be second

to the proprieties that instantly define
the state that's neither yours or mine.

Flashdance

Early reality a
dim, flat light,
incessantly the harbinger,
ever heralding the dawn,
suddenly transformed
to a new truth
by a brilliant burst,
illuminating and coloring
without and within,
imparting an indelible
glow reflected to
the farthest reaches,
continuously echoing
the lost lightning
long since dissipated,
fated to other realities.

Gwendolyn Park

Dance with me darlin', dance with me friend.
Press yourself on my heart in time without end,
merging bodies and souls into one,
a flight to the moon and beyond to the sun.

We joked and laughed and cautiously talked,
first sitting around and then as we walked
in measured, careful steps, self-conscious paces,
distance between us, but love on our faces.

We strolled through the day, and just after dark
were drawn to the lights of Gwendolyn Park,
where couples embraced as part of a dance,
lost in a music filled with romance.

Midst the scent of the flowers recently bloomed
I asked you to join me when the music resumed.
Your response was uncertain: "Yes, I'm inclined
if you tell me before what's on your mind."

While the music had played, it all seemed so clear:
to hold you, touch you and have you so near
that friends of the moment could deftly explore
if the fondness we felt could ever be more.

Silent fancied music, tangled in your head,
showed in your eyes a deep, haunting dread
I'd already decided to waltz you to bed,
ignoring my darlin' that you would've led.

I'm missing you now, as love on our faces
changed to a smile that simply erases
a moment in time with prospects galore,
now just a dream that might have been more.

Hands

A scudding cloud as passerby, hardly noticed.
Gentle wind, the passive wings of change.
That spot on my mind. The impression of your voice.
The moist small lips are smears at the entrance.
Your scent envelopes me, an intense hug.

Your hand a crevice that holds and strokes me.
Your touch is a patch, binding and healing.
A scudding cloud as passerby, hardly noticed.
Gentle blowing, the wispy wings of change.
That spot on my mind. The impression of your voice.
The moist small lips are smears at the entrance.
Your scent envelopes me, an intense hug.

Handsome

I watched your face
as your hand led me through
the gates of Paradise,
and your eyes were happy
and beautiful.

Heat of the Moment

It is now dark and rather cold
after a day that's been good,
filled with new ideas and with
love of the sweetest sort.
The tasks we shared were simple,
but they required the magic that
derives from being paired for
forty-seven years. I cannot
describe that magic, yet there
it was again. And I will look
for more tomorrow. That's
actually how we thrive and
ignore the dark and cold. In those
tasks I am yours, you're mine
and we *are*—beyond the moment.

Hello

For so long now
part of me has slept,
while the rest kept
pace with the "why" and "how"

of living and loving
as though the sleeping part
was never there, would never start
to the moving

force you have become.
You have stirred my soul,
given feeling to the whole
the once numb

portion denied.
The splendor of this feeling,
my mind and body reeling,
has wonderfully untied

the knots that bound
up and locked in the sweet, sublime
emotion, which in time
might come to be found

in the farthest reaches of
deep and requited love.

Heretofore

Small breaths passively drawn
while suffocating amidst foul air.

Wrong conclusions drawn
while seeking truth amidst nonsense.

Scribbles by artist drawn
while seeking reality amidst illusion.

"I love you," she said,
"I love you, I love you."

So, I said "I love you,"
her passion having drawn
the words from my mouth,
the minutes and hours suspended.

When we awoke,
time matched to the clock,
she urged me
not to focus
on just the one word.

High There

I was high today:
up there, out there,
because I was who I am—
for a while at least

I synthesized and propounded,
and I was quite astounded

afterwards by here and there
at the same time, by the tear

in the suffocating fabric
that has been the tragic

envelopment of my imagination.
I merely provided an explanation.

I merely shared what was on my mind,
though knowing it was the kind

of material available only from
me. I was not deaf and dumb.

I am not gone—just in abeyance.
I was happy again:
here in the now and then.

Homonyms

I am a currant.
A current defines where we go.
I am lost.

I Have Three Minutes

The moon is startling in the eastern sky
this night. I watched it move south on the sly

toward the Pacific Ocean, which it will never
reach, since the word, "toward," will ever

be a challenge to logic.

Incessant Shadows

As I lay abed, the room all dark,
thoughts fill my head to mark
my soul as a pox would scar my skin:
scar that locks out peace and torture in.

In the dark does my shadow live and play
until we join again in the light of day?

Is there sense in giving
life to a shadow as tho' it were living,
but not seen in the dark
as it is in the stark
brightness of day,
succinctly, black or gray?

One distressing shadow, one recurring thought
throws itself, dense and taut,
across my mind,
even in the blind
darkness bereft of truth.

Inertia 1

Señora, above all
remember that I love you,
that I am committed to what we have.
And remind yourself of momentum,
knowing that focus on the changing tides,
on the shifting sands
imprecisely detracts from what we know of
the constancy and beauty of the
sea and the dry, parched desert.

Inertia 2

Am I slower?
Or, are things faster?
There used to be a
temporal synchrony—
veritable lush symphony
where now wane cacophony
inserts from the periphery,
more a puzzle, a mystery,
neither fraternal nor sisterly,
nor a shout, just whispery
insertions. I long for the early
style, exertions from the pearly
inside—luminescent and smooth,
a reminder that now seems perfidy.
I am slow, but not yet inert.
That eventuates tomorrow.

Just above Reality

Your scarlet dress and raven hair
called out to challenge, to dare
me to touch your hand, quickly kiss
your lips, embrace you gently, or miss
forever the vibrant glow
we gradually came to know.
The truth about us hovers
just above reality, declaring
we've been sometime lovers,
but somehow always sparing
the alternative life
with the husband and wife,
the contextual domesticity
we need for social simplicity.

In 1980, a brilliant moonlit
October sky flooded Manhattan
as we walked about between
dance halls and bars, setting
a pattern for later years.
When we talked, bantering wit
became the medium of salty, lean
exchanges for carefully letting
go. When I thought we'd shifted gears
as we danced, the crisp satin
of your dress in this instance
put between us a staid distance.

Dallas in 1981 was another matter
as we would lollygag and chatter

in so many honkytonks and saloons,
changing our minds, becoming cartoons
in Stetsons and cowboy boots
dancing the Cotton Eye Joe in cahoots
with city-slicker geneticists
and veritable Texas cowboys
and cowgirls. Then stranger twists
as we shed our western toys
and went poolside where
the cautious did playfully dare
the carefree, among which I include
myself, to go swimming nude.

Detroit in 1982 was highlighted
by the Greek dives where we righted
whatever wrongs there might have been.
Blaring Motown music for dancing in
small places not meant for the crowd
of our number prompted us to shroud
ourselves in a world of our own.
And thus, the nature and tone
of our closeness began to change,
allowing us to explore and range
the full spectrum of our respective
lives, so that either could give
the other a focus and a hold
on life more intense and bold.
Finally, the music did stop,
leading us to seek the top
of the hotel, where in penthouse suite
we gathered in friendly effort to beat
our friends at poker. Then the jaded
left one by one as night faded
and only four of us were there
to greet the sun in its daily fare.

Norfolk in 1983 was tranquil,
a series of queries of "What will
we do?" We tried with some success
to hide our bored distress
by sharpened banter loaded
with sexual innuendo exploded
in the midst of droll, vacant
conversation as a nascent
friendship began to unfold
in ways yet to be told,
interrupted by my prior plan
to go directly to Japan.

Playful Toronto in 1984
was anything but a bore.
The playful goblins and ghosts
marking Halloween were among our
odd collection of hosts,
including costumes at cocktail hour,
like my grubby face mask,
causing us poignantly to ask,
"Just who are we?" The winner
of that contest sprang for dinner
at an intimate French restaurant,
where the query, "What do we want?"
was on everyone's mind.
Then the three of us left to find
the truth, first as haughty mavens
in a cozy wood-paneled bar,
and finally in the shadow of a star
or tunnels that serve as soft havens,
ultimately a vicarious bond
between us that is more than fond
memory: rather, the hand in glove
as simile for body in love.

Salt Lake City our meeting place
in '85, the first night a race
to find our mutual friend,
once and for always to end
the thirst and hunger that declare
our passions: to show that we care.
Remember how we rocked and rolled
in the lobby of the restyled old
Hotel Utah. Did we sing and dance.
Close enough that fancied romance
was not too far-fetched for
those who saw us. But, more
was to be told later, our pairing
merely an illusion, the more daring
challenge to propriety
left to fallacious notoriety.

Philadelphia in 1986 was disguise
for the surges the obliquely wise
would relegate to obscurity.
Together we sought security
in the revelations of computers
and other technical scooters
on which we propelled the present
into the future. You thoughtfully meant
to declare your professional pain
as coincidental, not the main
focus of life it'd become.
Yet, I knew. I sought to plumb
the silent, unnecessarily dumb
depths of your soul and combine
thereby what we were: yours and mine.

San Diego in 1987 was many
things and to forgive any

of them was hard for you, although
there were moments when we seemed to sow
so many oats: particularly after the formal
dance, when romping and stomping was normal
for even the staid among us; Roy
Schmickel I remember well. While the toy
that was our dancing failed to portend
the set of final steps that would end
his presence with us, for it I sorely miss
him. But, for you and me, there is the kiss
we never shared, others always intruding.
I remember your chagrin, even brooding
at the Fifties diner and after.
I know of no other time that laughter
was not *de rigueur* for you. Impressed
thereby, I tried to get us through a stressed
friendship (or more) and on to the party
in my room that brought the police at three
in the morning. For all of this I
apologize deliberately. The presence of my
friend from Milwaukee in one last trot
toward a single configuration that did not
abet her goals, leaving us with the query
of where we might go from here, still weary.

San Diego in 2007 offered one last chance
to resume and resolve our unfinished dance.
Twenty years ago we'd set in motion
a series of forces now circled full:
logic's softer push, passion's stronger pull,
passion returning like river to ocean.
No dormant, inert seed, the central core
we nurtured then has always been my seething
focus for engagement, natural as breathing;
a comfortable background promising more,

yet held back, kept in check. And above
me tonight a full moon brilliantly burns
in a final checkmate as it ironically turns,
making final whimsy of our long-lost love,
those desultory moments when we were one
of heart and of soul, forever just begun.

Late-Sunday Afternoon

The sun is perched on the edge of my day—
like my life is positioned in mankind.
In a few moments, the day will be dark,
the dark not yet a harbinger of nothing,
rather a casual interval, leaving the drama
of finality indeterminate. But, more than yesterday
there is an aura, a faint glow that allows me
to be aware of what my corporeal senses miss.
Nonetheless, I am at peace and my life is sated
as I ponder the nature of cycles.

Lew's First Fellow

It has been forty years since I met Lew.
He was cramped in an office where the two

of us could sit, but not breathe a whole lot,
let alone talk, but we did—of my plot

to rise in academics on the rocket of DNA,
studying genes and babies so that one day

we would change the world. He liked it just fine
but declared "the decision's not mine.

To fellow at MGH is up to John."
I slept on these words and at the next dawn

was told by the boss he did quite agree
with Lew but had no funds. "I'll do it for free,"

I declared and began later that year:
first the clinic, then lab, all in good cheer,

with amino acids, cell culture, birth defects
and chromosomes, and then the effects

of one special gene that leads to skin tumors,
but wasn't well known in spite of the rumors

that it was common. Lew sensed a spark
and admonished me to bring from the dark

the secrets of NF, to stop my carousin':
outdo that dude von Recklinghausen.

Lord's Prayer in Omes

Our Genes that art in cells,
hallowed be Thy name.
Thy kingdom come. Thy will be done
in tissues as it is in species.
Give us this day our daily DNA
and forgive us our mutations
as we remove those who mutate amongst us.
And lead us not into mutagenesis,
but deliver us from mutant alleles.
For Thine is the Genome,
the Epigenome and the Proteome
forever and ever. Amen.

Love as Voussoir

The substance of our love is
continuous if your presence is not.
The substance of our reality is
in moments not defined by time.

The reality of love is
the insertion of one life
into another, the binding
wedge transcending time.

Love as a Desert Flower

Over time that seems forever,
complacent breezes ironically push
and displace the final bits of life
from monotonous pale sand,
parched and barren. The promise
of brightly colored scented petals,
of verdant lushness a mirage,
an illusion, except when errant
clouds in heavy torrents
share their essence with
hidden, tenacious seeds.

But unlike the oasis,
I have known only
the promise of the promise,
the sun shower that merely
awakens and readies
a dormant kernel,
the incomplete plight
that bodes and harkens,
but leaves to another day
the shoot and bloom.

Love Is One

We have shared two rivers, you and I,
each to be recalled in terms of raging torrents,
wonderfully pummeling and cascading;
or, perhaps as seen from another eye,
as gently mixing, eddying currents
quietly, yet completely pervading

my senses and entire being
so that what was once sublimely shared
has become the metaphor to provide
the basis for knowing or seeing
the nature and substance of what we dared
and ultimately I cannot hide

from myself: The waters of those two
rivers have inextricably mixed
and become one. And so, it is that you
and I have come to see the both of us fixed
into a singular reality of
deep and most satisfactory love.

Mask

I am walking the stark desert of Najd.
Your presence in my reverie is
as strong as the sun's relentless
rays transforming my face.
A pleasant intense warmth,
a taut flush, a delicate invisible
mask uniting us: my face
buried in your being,
your being part of my reality.

Last December in Montreal, as
I walked from my hotel to yours,
my breath and a light snow in a soft wind
combined into a similar mask. That
glowing tension and tingling pressure then
mixed with the pulsing of our hearts
as we talked about your music.

The swelling within and the pleasure on
my cheeks and lips merged as a sensation
to savor long after you'd gone. But
alone again in my hotel room, in
just the time I spent removing my coats
and tie, the gentle warmth there
undid the magic and took you from me.

So, I am loath to enter now
the damp coolness of a stony
catacomb to lose you once again.

Melding

Globular bursting raindrops
push between and surround
moon-drenched stones,
impervious, resistant
to mingling and confluence.

Two elements forcing,
resisting the other without
contest, more a matter of gravity,
quarks, indifference, or other
intense powers; distinction
and interface paramount.

But what of melding, a deliberate
or insouciant unity deriving
from the mélange that defines us?

I am the pebbles of the bed.
You are the stream's water
that flows through me,
taking part of me with you.
You are the sand at the ocean's shore.
I am the sea that does more
than impinge; I completely explore
and occupy the interstices
that are as much a part
of you as the grains,
the silica, the granite,

of your igneous substance.
You are a dune of sand.
I am the soft Spring rain
that permeates and
becomes one with you again.

Mess of Tangles

The glory of cats is that
they're ever curious, always at

the window of a new introduction
into life's charms, a seduction,

really, inviting steps where
there have been none; one more square

in the geometric puzzle of life, a mess
of tangles that are not a source of distress.

Rather, curiosity is our glory, too, love
of what's unknown, a shrine to what we're of.

The unknown does not deny us. We simply are:
the present forever, near and afar.

Midday Sun

The dew glistens,
    then dries
as the sun rises
    and I become aware
of you again. In synchrony,
a sun also rises in my soul,
though I have the sense
there will not be nearly
as many new ascents. This
is simply part of becoming
the absence we all
    eventually are.

Moon

Twenty years ago, we set in motion
a series of forces now circled full:
passion's softer push, logic's stronger pull.
But passion returns, like river to ocean.

No dormant, inert seed, the central core
expanding now has always been our seething
focus for engagement, natural as breathing;
a comfortable background promising more,

yet held back, kept in check. But above
us tonight the Sap moon brilliantly burns,
overcoming the logic as it magically turns
us on to each other in unbridled love.

Moon Song

Dawn of our day begun with thin cloud
hanging close, a misty silver shroud;

by noon transformed to dappled scudding,
and bright blue illuminating faces in budding

love. Then sunset's clearing; gently blazing
reflected, slanting light on snow, amazing

slopes all white just below the ridge
forming a momentary supernatural bridge.

Finally, moon rose full above the mountain
peaks to present a bold and magic fountain

of light and earth; something beyond our "yes" and "no."
We sensed it soft on our faces and souls, like so

many elements deep within that resonated
with its song of a trio reinstated

in silent joyful full-voiced chorus;
a lifting communion, sung by and for us.

Moonkiss

You woke me this morning.
Sharing the time with you
I walked among the trees,
the moon's breath kissed my cheek
and you were there,
told me what we knew,
and I said I love you.

There are some truths that
serve where facts do not—
your presence this morning,
our love yesterday and tonight;
you are my light, my force.

This love we have
is my most sacred truth.

More than a Number

Is being alive
at seventy-five
worth celebrating
or are devastating
functions and facts
at play—for example, pacts
with the Devil's minions?
I seek broader opinions
to resolve my quandary.
Was I just dirty laundry
or something more akin
to a desultory spin
on the problematic—
like a duped asthmatic
whose treatment inhaler
works more like a jailer
locking me into a cell
commensurate with Hell?

No! My current plight
is actually "just right."
While there was conundrum,
I've able to add and sum
complex factors of my life,
with sweet help from my wife:
to exact a happy time on earth
in the time since my birth.
I'm happy to be here now,
tho' I can't say just how.
And keying off the present

does not conger or invent
the joy I do experience.
It's like quantum decoherence
that accounts for reality
based on a technicality
most of us don't understand.
My life's been much more grand
than the details might suggest,
so, I'll just say that "I am blessed."

More than Bumps

She came to me with her son,
a mother concerned about his bumps
and dark spots, darker even than
the surrounding dark skin
that had already diminished him
in a lightly pigmented world.

I pressed on about her own bumps
and she directed me to behind
her right knee. A few days
later we separated her from her knee,
leaving a short brown stump
connected to her hip. She did well
and was happy when I visited her

twenty-five years later—after her son
had died from the same transformation
of one of his bumps. "NF," she lamented.
Not funny – not at all! Yet, her son
and extremity gone, she still found fun—
the joy of being alive and whole of person.

And then a final bump the unwitting
surgeon stumbled on and in,
draining her life from her—
and her spots and her bumps and her husband.
She was not perfect, but she was more . . .
a good woman and mother and wife.

I was asked to make some sense of her demise,

because I knew the spots and the bumps
were not who she was and that they were
no detraction from her and no excuse
for her absence. We all miss her . . .
except maybe the surgeon.

Near Miss

Texas 71 between
Columbus and Austin
is sometimes boring,
sometimes a challenge:
LaGrange a test and
lament from the past,
while Alum and Plum
are in cahoots with the radio,
which is where I find you
these days. There you are,
there we are, the music
recalling the best and worst
of who we were together.

Replace the radio
with Texas monotony
and in the silence our
love makes its own music,
though this time as
a lingering memento,
not the compelling
focus for the future
the songs declare.

I do love you,
knowing the past
to be no less
our treasure for
its capture there.

Never-Ending Moments

1st

Soothing flight.
Soul tranquil.
Mind focused,
intense with science;
presentation honed.
New Mexico an unknown
(Santa Fe briefly removed from Albuquerque).
Your presence polite gesture, casual,
but electric, burgeoning;
the drive adumbrating.
Perfunctory tasks at college,
domestic meal and required conversations,
musical libations and social incantations
mix and swell. As we dance
our centers merge, ignite.
Under enchanted moon,
river's grass cool on our skin
as flames grow.

2nd

Presentation polished, well-received,
then slow, exhausting data.
Finally, displacement to a new reality.
Tour of old city and new;
quietude of Tesuque:
baptism, resurrection, brimstone skies.

Collapse in reverie, love a soporific.
As the moon rises, new and old friends meet;
music and communion, thunder and lightning.

3rd

Sleep gives perspectives; plans by phone.
Endure the morning science.
Agonize through lunch with colleagues.
Then walk through Santa Fe,
sampling places and spirits,
parading and declaring ourselves.
One, the moviemaker, saw and knew.
Pretending at a goddess' feet,
then dinner, eventually five of us,
metaphysics and art foremost.
At moon's peak, bodies in unison,
hearts merged, sensibilities one,
the truth palpable as a new reality.

4th

Dawn integral to final minutes:
beyond respite to indelible
branding of souls, hearts
with each other's being;
sweet merging again
as songbirds cheer us
and hoot owls portend
a languishing return
through Albuquerque
to an alternative,
earlier beginning.

5th

This time thirst, hunger,
aching expectations;
San Francisco together begins
as sun submerges offshore.
Victorian manor's special offering,
the Morning Room, your first gift.
Second, my life and future
muraled and baked in clay.
Face smiles, heart races,
hidden tears crescendo.
I am yours.

6th

Hazy early-morning sun
reflected, multiplied;
aura of a morning room mirroring us.
Thirsts slaked, hearts rest;
time for syllogisms, new discoveries.
Later, rewarded, smug; day fruitful,
fretful (you are sorely missed).
Day's end begins with your return:
dinner blends stratified friendships,
colors of art, sounds of music
and words of science.
Day's end a fact
in a moonlit morning;
room aglow, crescendos matched.

7th

Slow arousal, unhurried
breakfast in bed

befitting Victorian elegance;
room's magic continues.
Cable car: nostalgic ride
or life's ups and downs
in narrow trajectories?
Buena Vista Irish coffees
mellow perspectives. Damp fog;
scents of fish, brine, creosote,
busy tourists; gulls playing tag
starboard aft; windswept view
of Golden Gate's belly.
Soft, warm rain *en route* to
Museum of Fine Arts.
Return to the Haight,
perfect place for old vinyl music.
Late afternoon embraces our room
where we enfold each other in weary peace.
Renewed, Little Italy for repast and new friends;
were they really brother and sister?
Dancing in space measured by elbows,
embers glow, your heat palpable,
clothing drenched.
We slow and cool off
listening to music of an airplane
returned to an old haunt.
Unhurried yet, the moon waning,
our words renew one pact,
our bodies begin another.

8th

Church bells herald the day;
muted chimes, subdued light,
tempered passion, tender deliberateness,
even constraint:

apparent finality of distance,
a barrier looming just hours away,
subdues us both.
But, awash in love,
we pursue our realities in each other.
We are reality.
At the edge of California
in a cliff house,
obvious beginning and sustenance
of innumerable realities,
my peace and joy unprepared
for the tears we both know
about today's end:
rushing tide, gentle ebbing.
Then crashing surf on rocks below
declares my temerity,
love no longer a footnote,
nor enclosed in parentheses.
In our final moments
briny sweet tears again,
echoing the surf,
joining the ocean, rivers, streams
posited as substance of our love
so that now we know
distance as an illusion.
Today cannot end.

Nonstop

There we were,
molecules of water
packaged as snowflakes,
mixed and coalesced,
shaped by love's goddess
into a snowball,
a perfect communion,
but then left casually
to melt, to puddle and
evaporate, displaced from
each other to the world
of in between for so long.

Until now, as I sense you
somewhere in the distance,
molecules racing toward
each other to mingle again
in a mist of two sweet
breaths, merging as a
droplet, finally knowing
who we are.

Now and Again

Now that we have finally met,
remind me of our times together,
our steps and paths often
one as we've wandered
each other's lives.

Do you remember Carmel,
Santa Fe, or 1987?
And the sun's blush
as we touched, the scent
of oranges as we walked away?

Fragile truths and your
presence in this instant
now portend and again
recall our reality.

Oasis

My face buried in your hair,
our breasts and loins aroused,
joined as by magnets
while our feet and hearts
merge three rhythms and
magically the feral instincts
and the social terpsichore
transform the instant into
both the momentary nidus
and the continuum that merges time
with the reality of our passions,
the fantasies of our reality.

That we have been together
in other guises, in other
settings along this warp
is one more way to say that
our reality together did not
just begin, even as we know
we are isolating ourselves
in the specific transformation
of coming together as the seed
for the crystal, the swelling
of the spiral. Again
the dormant seed becomes
an oasis, a haven,

a soft presence in the now
of the titillating future
we will be and have been.

Our love is unending and timeless
as the reality of our passions,
now so urgently declared.

October 25

We had only one thing planned—
Sue's colleagues had a grand

celebration for the twenty-five
years she applied moxie and drive

to enhance the well-being and health
of CIGNA clients through her vast wealth

of nursing wherewithal. From bedpans
to "digital patients," her know-how spans

the full gamut, affording a patient-centered
approach, from once the patient entered

a system otherwise depersonalized,
a system wherein she long ago realized

was short on heartfelt compassion.
She pours out her love in a fashion

that both keeps the sick patient alive
and lets a sick health industry thrive.

Ode to an Oh So Laden Bin

People in some configurations are Muslim.
Cotton in some configurations is muslin,

a valued fabric I store in a special bin
that now is fully laden, topped to the brim.

But why do I covet this cotton so?
After all, muslin, as you obviously know,

is readily available from many vendors
who profit from its feel and other splendors.

So why do I see instead a Muslim bin laden
rather with silken cloth for a dancing maiden?

Once

Summer is not Fall, one trailing on the other.
Once, caught up in a very special Summer,
someone warned me of Fall's travails.
I faltered and looked ahead instead
of declaring that Summer's wonder,
not realizing the sequence is mere distraction.

Once, a wondrous wine
I took as preface
and stopped drinking of it
for fear of what would be.
But that already was and is,
and the nectar is gone.

One Beginning

Your friend made it clear:
you were a woman I should know.
We started out on moonlit snow
over the seven springs where

fantasies formed and merged
in talk of cream and brandy,
of fun and pleasure randy,
as each the other gently urged

to seek a deeper, more intense
engagement. Which we did in July,
an enduring promise to try
to give some final sense,

to nurture and gently fashion
our blossoming world,
the flower sublimely unfurled
by requited love and passion.

I dare not recount
each expression and test
of that love, the worst and best
adding or removing some amount

that belies the wonderful sum
of what we together did become.

Orange Glow

As I awoke, I heard the ring
and snap of the bedspring;

then cold feet made a tired floor creak,
and finally, the rusty squeak

of the kitchen door hinge
while a fresh orange

gave up its scent as you sliced
it and so ritually spiced

our early-morning show
with a kind of golden glow.

Pastels in a Dream

I know you like to
paint: then, to soften
a single, silly stone
standing hard, alone;
now, to tame
the wild self-same soul
frantic 'neath my breast!
but numbed to rest
in every other part.

You rendered my heart
like you softened the stone
so that it'd grown
and roused itself from wild
solitude to befit a child
who knows of
naught but love.

Paths

Path 1

On only several days of the year
does the sun rudely violate my cell:
a slender beam that seems to tear
the dark, shatter the silence, dispel

the knowledge that I am everything.
Today it's a spotlight traversing the wall,
now resting a moment on a spider's ring
of webbing that sparkles again' the pall,

the spokes and cross-pieces deploying
like roads and paths on a map.
I study it, recollecting, then destroying
it before it fills the blank gap

between who I am and what I've done.
Had anyone seen it, my before
and after would have begun
to make sense to those keeping score

of the heads and hands and feet
that I have disassembled
and relished as my special treat:
as they suffered, I shook and trembled

with raw, soaring, fulfilling lust.
They'd ventured on the paths and roads
that were only mine to wander: just
go. Just do it. The map bodes

and hearkens, with no need to choose
one way at the price of another,
nothing to win, nothing to lose.
Just do it. No constraint of choice to smother

what I am, who I am, a lone, sublime
traveler with no need to choose, to care
what is right and what's left, no time
to decide, to think, to feel, to share.

Path 2

My bare feet soft on the wooded trail,
our fingers intertwined as you walked
beside me, our hearts one as we talked
about our lives joined in that frail

communion of newfound love.
As dawn broke this morning, my plan
was to leave unnoticed, as a man
is wont to do, looking beyond or above

what we had shared; to strike
another route more familiar and free
from having to decide for two, and just be
myself. But you awoke and, quite like

in a dream, returned me to your side
to begin again the sweet and captivating
engagement we'd been celebrating
for hours before. I could not hide

my pleasure, nay, the rapture
that swelled as together we came

to conclude we'd walk as one in the same
path, joined so that each might capture

the being of the other. Thus, did we dare
to choose what only they who love
always have available: the constraint of
passion derived from what we share.

Patient Waiting

I was in the exam room because
I was in pain. A lot of pain.
Occasionally the doc looked up
from his laptop—I presume
to see if I was there. I'd spent more
time in the waiting room than with him.

But the waste had just begun. "Go
to the third floor for blood tests and
then to the basement for X-rays." The
door to the lab facility challenged my
compromised strength and worsened the
pain. But I had over an hour to recover—
a harbinger interval. The wait in X-ray
was even longer. Patients are now simply
sources of specimens and data—and income.

Poem, March 2020

The photographs capture what was now
of then. They make known not just that, but how

we have a basis for continuing
the reality of the winnowing

of one into the other. One after
the first is the second, but the laughter

makes it seem like the third or even fifth
as the speed ramps up and brings quickly with

it an urgency that does contradict
what I have shared with you in the conflict

that is going on and on until you tell
me "enough is enough—just go to hell."

Poemless

Reflecting on our last meeting,
I realized no one would ever write
a love poem about you, entreating
you to hold dear and tight

the love oft and sweetly proffered.
For, when all is said and done,
no matter the manner the love is offered,
the tale of being loved has never begun

for you. There is that simple admonition
to "let somebody love you" you cannot heed,
a private overwhelming premonition
allowing love in words, but never deed.

Poetry

The words and the sounds have slipped by me
as though either they or their true or false
concoctions were irrelevant or not
appreciated by my eyes or ears.

In any event, there was no input
and therefore no "pictures of thoughts" as the
Austrian philosopher declared of them.
I have studied his understanding of
language since 1961 and am
that much the better for it. He makes clear
that "language disguises thought" and therefore
we can trust neither one of these brain tools.

"It's all about games." Word games are the source
of where we go from here—this rule, that rule
is how we sort it out. The rules are so clear—
why else would they be rules—blue is cyan
and rose is red and oxygen is life.
And my sister is Barbara as is
oft repeated by a relative who knows.

Presence

I can't believe how much I miss you.
You are not here to hear, to know
the joy I have because of you. I do
miss you, the way you surrounded me.

I have tried to divine my life without you.
On the one hand, that's impossible: you've
been my life for so many years.
Yet, you're not here: it is possible.

How am I possible without you?

Confounding Loss

I just had a nice conversation
with my longtime friend, a situation
we are often happy about when the
results are laughable and go to a
smooth and polished clear-cut finality
that declares truth and reveals finality.

But I have begun a memory loss
so that I wonder if I really can
share all that I was as a nuanced man,
who was once both a servant and the boss.

Princesses of Chengdu

Long shadows from the bright sun
highlighted the talking, walking, biking throngs
along the lower south side of the Jin Jiang
River as I returned from likely one

of my most fulfilling perambulations.
And the adventure had only begun.
Three princesses, Rose, Violette and Jung,
inquired of my native articulations.

"Do you speak English?" the soft-spoken query.
It seemed this royal trio had grown weary

of learning grammar and pronunciation
from their local teachers and had sought conversation

more cosmopolitan. And fickle chance
engaged us as a quartet to dance

in words and rhyme: a noble quest
to show that everything happens for the best.

Promises Displaced

Woman, where have we gone;
what have we done
with our talents and strengths?
To what consummate lengths
have we forced, pushed, pressed
the abilities that could be addressed
to the issues at hand?

I am weak, supercilious and
in need of a focus, a goal;
something, anything to make whole
the rag-tag fragments and parts
of the patchwork of starts
and promises for the future displaced
by the compulsively retraced
errors and disturbances of the past.

Perhaps now, at long last,
we, or even I, can stay
what had seemed the inevitable way,
and proceed to take to task
the answer to what we ask
of ourselves again and again.

Puzzle

I love jigsaw puzzles. They take a while,
but the completed picture can both beguile

and exhilarate. You start by defining the limits
with the edge pieces, the sum of which permits

you to consider and build towards the center,
where the converging pieces begin to enter

another reality, each specifically conforming
to rigid physical rules, terrifically performing

optical tricks as the isolated component
merges with others in the defining moment
when we realize forever, not just now.

I love life. I like to stroke it, gently nuzzle
it and coax it so that it's less a puzzle

that demands you must start at the distant
edge to enhance it centripetally, resistant

to my reaching out across some border
of fancied reality, some rule that will order

us into oblivion. Life after all is simply turmoil
and chaos that will not dissipate or roil
when we realize forever, not just now.

Recursive Now

What is love? Multiple events
or processes, maybe even
clustered memories embedded
in the heart? My friend no
longer has any recourse to
recent memories, for they
are long gone. But he is madly
in love—not just any time. Rather
now. Only now. Day after day
he falls in love with her, cherishing
it on the instant. Not a piece
or fragment of then, but recursive
now. Can there be better love,
that exquisitely boiling soul,
day after day? Surely his lover
is also very pleased.

Reification

For so long I have contrived a delicate
balance, ever adjusting to approximate

a semblance of peace and quietude
within. Till now it has been attitude

merely, that is posture, inclining
this way or that, delicately divining

the proper sum of forces about the fulcrum.
But, with you here the sense of conundrum

has faded. The pivot point or focus
has transmuted from a critical locus

to a broad and comfortable base,
a casual plane that is now a welcome place

from which to experience and explore
a world that had previously been more

the riddle or mystery than a treasure
of love or any other happy measure
that your presence has brought to my life.

Respite

The quiet is loud
sometimes and will crowd

the space of music
we all use to trick

the brain to pretend
that there is no end.
For music will bend

the seam of space-time—
with or without rhyme—

into the 'morrow
where we cannot go
otherwise. So, altho'

musical sounds are brief
bring they sweet relief.

Rhapsody

Everything that makes sense to me now
derives from you; even your slightest
innuendo sends ripples grown to waves
I know as silent, tender impressions on
my heart and soul, my being. Please,
keep at it forever, as this is always
how I want us to be, alternative
renderings of the same reality,
mystical interdigitations and forces
arranging and rearranging our energies in
never-ending blissful harmony.

Precious, cherished woman, always
will I care, no matter what,
visions of you constantly providing
new vigor and new directions to how I
imagine the ways we spend time together,
nuzzling, cuddling, stroking, touching,
kissing as prelude and in afterglow.

Rich Heart

I write with the name Biscardi,
but ultimately, I am a Riccardi,

a man of the rich heart,
who tells tales that start

as Eden's garden begins
its confounding of sins

and devotion. I am of
the heart rich in love

and tell tales that end
yesterday or maybe bend

into tomorrow—"now"
and "before," "you" and "thou"

simply different ways
the bow smartly plays

my heart's strings. To be rich
is not to have to switch

from one point in time
to another: a sublime

presence in whenever,
the past but a clever

illusion; the future
an imperfect suture

hemming reality
to the ticking of finality.

Sap Moon

Perigee moon intense keen light
reflecting off snow pristine white

illuminates your smiling face
revealing love and tender grace.

In those moments we are one:
our hearts, our souls, forever just begun.

Saturday, 12-13-14

It won't happen again for
a thousand years or so:

The year's month number
followed by the month's date,
which is one more than
the month number, and one
less than the ultimate
two digits of the present year.

Does it matter? A day is a day.
But I note it with some pleasure
and the pleasure matters. It's
a signpost that somehow makes
more sense than most other
clues to life. At the least, there
is a pattern, a formula beyond
the canons that have failed us.

Shafts

The clouds gather 'round this mountain,
shedding what seem to be fitful tears,
sharing how sad we are that you're not here.
Not here to know the love that seethes
within as the storm mirrors my passion:
lightning, turgid shafts of electric forces
eliciting exquisite sighs and shudders;
thunder, extended shafts of sound
resonating in your chamber.

Snow Rhyme

I hurried by the window
and saw the snow.

You had the time
to mingle and rhyme

with that bright
and promising white.

You took the time
to sing me that rhyme;

I heard to know
we shared the snow.

Softhaven

I have known your softness
and your peace,
and in that haven,
that quintessential stillness
we quietly shared,
I have found the crease
in the warp of heaven
for those who would have dared
to go beyond,
to feel and live
the truth that is the bond
between now and forever.
You cannot give
me more, ever.

Some Time

We've tried for some time,
both ostentatious and sublime,

to derive one ultimate sensation

along with which we can store—
still and serene, not the gore

as sometimes is the case,
like when a beautiful face

reveals more without makeup.
A catastrophic shake-up

allowing the stark existential
within the expanding potential

of trapped energy, soon to explode
into utter reality that does bode

the truth affording self-revelation.

Song in Silence

With a full heart to sing quietly
is to wait for her
with patience to bring quietly
what she would prefer,

knowing full well that what she brings,
be it gift or her,
will give me voice, as my heart sings
so softly to her.

Start of Something New

The sun rises, initiating a new day.
But the day isn't new—it's really
just another day in an old cycle.
The new day for earth was when it
began to rotate near the sun and
nobody was here to appreciate it.
So, what is new in these regards?

At age 75, what's new for me? My
death? For others, death might be
new, but I've died several times before,
only to be successfully resuscitated.
I want another new! How about a poem
about something new, with "new" in the
title? It is new—enough to make me happy.

Still Too Many Words

The term, explication, epitomizes
or, some might rightly say, disguises

my involvement in life. I articulate
where others might smile or gesticulate

merely. At least until our respite
of summer, that ultimately divined night

when I could no longer simply resort
to words, the exchange much more than a report.

Because of your silently declared love
I am finally able to proceed above

and beyond words, words, words. I am in love,
and for the first time at that. (Although of

course we are left with the meaning of "first."
And, oh, here, as in the past, is my worst:

digression in words from the real heart
of the matter, rather than live the part
that is the crux of it after all.)

I love you with a love wending far beyond
the instant, to where the magic wand

takes us and I finally know a wonderment,
a peaceful, profound, unspoken rapture.

I love you, a truth that does enthrone
me as the magic King whose life and love
are yours to have and share.

Sunrise

Night's journey done,
a sliver of brilliance
at water's edge
quietly and indelibly marks
with sweet magnificence
the insertion of one
life into another,
a binding wedge.

Owls and sleepy larks
retire and the other
fantasy of rolling stream,
alive in a tenacious dream
a signal of enduring love,
merges once more
with the wispy reality of
communion at the shore.

Taken

I'm here.
But I want to be somewhere else
at the same time.
That's what we lose,
what we've lost.
I can't be taken
to another part of me,
to another part of us.
That kind of me is gone.
I want to be somewhere else:
not instead, but also.
Else. Also.

Time was, music could take me there—
not a place—just somewhere else.
Something else, someway else.

In this chair, my mind in the music,
in an embrace,
unity a fiction, not a
temporal truth.
Time is different now.
Two of us at the same time—
merely our own times.
I want us to be one
in a time neither
yours nor mine.

Music used to take me there.
You used to take me there.
And just now, for a moment,
as I wrote this, I was there,
lingering, clinging.
But I'm back now.
Not waiting;
just knowing
it was not, is not.

The feel of happy is different.
But happy.
Happy, one at a time,
only here, not also there.

Tales of the Pup's Wagging Tail

Now I will tell you the story of Urs,
born in February of a doc and a nurse.

She has a great skill, unique to her kind:
she gets you to do what she'd been assigned.

If in the womb this skill she had plied,
believe me, my friends, she'd still be inside.

But, out she did come and said to the midwife,
"Here's a hundred bucks to buy me a good life."

So, Peanuts, in addition to the love that you sought,
know in the end that you have been bought.

But, now she's reformed, adoring your bark,
as your most rapid tail does away with the dark.

Tender Mercies

I done it right and I done it wrong.
Ugly drinkin' and purty song.

A kinda lovin' that only satisfies
for the moment, stories and lies.

But then you said for me to stay
here with you and your boy. Your way

to share your love, to sweetly, gently render
a broken man whole through mercies tender.

The Answer

It was a mystery:
the lumberjack asked,
"Where did the log go?"

Repeating history,
the judge was tasked,
"Where did the law go?"

To answer them all,
I put in a call
to my friend, Nick Felago.

The End

The end of the day or the night
or the week, even the year—
or a life, your life. What do we think of
or do we want? A name or description
is not the usual response. And certainly
not the desired one. How does the end play out?

It's now the end of the day, that is,
the first of February 2020. I'm tired
and in a lot of pain. What's next? Is it
really the end? Or just a transition? What's the
difference between terminus and nexus? I think I
know—or did at one time. One is a time for leaving
and one's for sleeping. I am not tired, so I shan't yet
sleep. And where's my pain from? The pain

is a long story. Too long for right now of course—
unless all you want to do is sleep. My wife
is right here, keeping her eyes on me! "Be careful"
she says again and again. Make sure I fit like I
used to. If I fell in head first we'd both be in trouble.
Butt-first would be a challenge, too. How about "Heart first?"
Can you do that? Can you lead with your heart if'n you're
my partner? Or NOT my partner? My horse's eyes have
tears in them. Some of them may be mine. Fudge! Heck.

Tomorrow we'll set this straight—unless I wake early.

The Plane Beyond

The Russian likened her
to a dawning, with
new light and colors
effecting a beginning
not otherwise possible for him.
I want to sing the same
praises for you,
for from your presence
all things, myself especially,
have a new meaning,
a hitherto unknown glow.
But, alas, I am no such poet:
I am all too well aware
of my own dark perceptions
and your righteous uncertainty;
and I am too literal,
meticulously describing and arranging
where the poet perceives and responds
from the heart.

I know of love.
But I am cold, above
or, if you will, below
that which most would know
as the plane
wherein we sustain
the warmth, the fire,
that unbridled desire

bespeaking, extolling
the wandering, rolling
force that pushes,
presses or rushes
the feeling.

The Way Back

I entered your life broken and alone,
hurling in mad drunken fury along
an angry self-destructive one-way track.

Through your love I've changed and gently grown
to know those tender mercies writ in song
so sweet, I turned around and came back.

Thou

I think on thee
and wish to be
in thy tender midst,
gently known, softly kissed.

I remember your face
as your hand led me through
the Gates of Paradise,
and your eyes were happy
and beautiful.

Threads

I am uncertain of how many years
we have chanced the laughter and the tears,

knowing each other as lovers and friends,
a mélange of secret moments that blends

so many truths that some are blithely left
unnoticed; simply put, truth bereft

of knowledge. Then yesterday, for the first
time I saw from your vantage point in a burst

of new images. Specifically,
a repeated sequence of carefully

woven patterns in the sum of your own
experience, and what I should have known

all along. I'm a series of discrete
dangling threads available for repeat

insertions into the lovely substance
that is the fabric of your life; to dance

with you, provide a focus, a highlight.
Intensely gratifying. But what might

be better from your own perspective
is not a patchwork of interruptive

threads. Rather, one area large and growing
from a continuous thread without slowing.

Time Demand and Momentum

What to do with the time left me? Doesn't
make any difference how much. Am I just biding time?
How much vigor when there are goals? Is there
still time to make a difference? And how much
difference? Am I kidding myself? Is it nothing
more than routine, my life always determined
by goals? How much do I really want to do what
I am doing? Is it more than momentum, and if so,
how'd I come to know that?

Titillation

Not quite rain,
the finest mist
most softly kissed
the flushed skin
of my face,
a sweet embrace
deriving sublime
and mystical force
(like a subtle rhyme
drawing words together
in a poem), a source
of delicate passion,
a wispy feather
stroking in a fashion
that brings touch to titillation.

To Dr. R.

As a child, my hands were small
and fine, my skin was smooth and clear.
As a teen I stood proud and tall,
a person of peace and hope and cheer.
My darlin' treats me right.
But, when I'm pushed away,
hurt by what people say,
thrown alone into the night
I look to you to find
love of another kind.
Then I saw a second script begin
as darkened spots showed on my skin,
like shadows cast by a bright
sun on small clouds, blocked light
heralding the dread and storm,
arrived as fleshy hillocks, a form
of exploding, erupting fountains
soon grown to looming mountains.
My darlin' treats me right.
But, when I'm pushed away,
hurt by what people say,
thrown alone into the night
I look to you to find
love of another kind.
My hands are not mine anymore,
painful in clasping and holding,
distorted by those mountains sore;
they have been my despair, a scolding
nightmare, while you've been my hope,
helping me see beyond suffering, the taunt

the tease, the burden with which I cope.
But my heart aches most for want
of mine, the children who never were
for fear of mountains and the shadows.
My darlin' treats me right.
But, when I'm pushed away,
hurt by what people say,
thrown alone into the night
I look to you to find
love of another kind.
And my heart aches most for want
of mine who never were,
for fear of mountains and the shadows.

To Sue on Returning from Work

I have, by God,
removed my bod'

from off this bed
where in my stead
you'll lay your head;

to sleep and dream,
that it might seem

a pleasant, tiny time
twixt reading this rhyme
and the pleasure sublime
of your heart next to mine.

To Taste Responsibility

Loving,
living
is savoring
wine unblemished.
My tarnished
cup
fills up
and quickly
adds the garnish
of that tarnish:
so sickly.

But with my soap,
responsibly,
I hope
fervently
to preen
and clean
that flask.
I ask
only,
humbly,
that this tongue
of mine
touch
pure wine.

The taste
of soap
residual

adds gradual
to waste
more the wine
and breaks ope'
my heart.
Thus, I start,
again, to know
there is no
loving,
living
for me.

Truth as Perspective

One Time

Three colors splattered,
as if it mattered,
on canvas coarse.
They scream, bold and hoarse,
of things all wrong.
No room for song
and tender truth.

Another Time

On these three colors scattered
to show they mattered
I looked and saw,
and wept with awe
to see them sing
and gently bring
to me the tender truth.

Truths and Color

I could tell you why the sky is blue:
I'd outline the facts in terse
prose or render lilting verse.
But only one depicts what's true.

We've learned over time
soft, singing rhyme,
not reason, derives
the truths of our lives.

It seems precision detracts.
What purpose there be
is known not by facts
but another reality.

Two Becomes Everything

The river of Life
that is not life nor alive,
seaward flows:
To live one goes
from sea to source.

The journey on
its placid, almost-still course
wearies to the bone,
while on the quick, white water,
not alone,
a richness grows
as he rows.
And she, too.

The journey is inane,
but all the same
two together
become everything:
by rhyme, not reason,
actually, especially
through white water.

United Airlines Flight 175

Juliana, I was to pick you up
at the airport in Los Angeles.
But something went wrong
and you are no more.
Juliana, I loved you,
most precious child.

My daughter's gift of you
a meeting of tame and wild
reality to become the future,
our togetherness a beguiled
synthesis of having fun and truth.
You plunged to death, as a stewardess dialed
her phone to say evil was ending your youth.

Wasted Time

We refer to "wasted time" as though
the time was like the coins lost from a hole
in your pants pocket. Gone. It ain't no more
within your reach. Really what is wasted
are your efforts during that time period.

You can't lose time like you can lose quarters.
Time has no comparable metallic
reality. And we equate effort
and metal with time—an illusion that
gives a substance to time that really is
nonsense. Sorta like declaring that "time
flows"—like a stream or a river flows.

Did you ever get soaking wet from time?

When Not Accounts for Nott

We came together in the second grade
in Nineteen-Forty-Seven, after I made

the game-changing journey from East to West,
leaving Brooklyn so as to know the best

of Southern California first hand.
The teacher, Mrs. Strong, made us all feel grand,

so the three of us—Nott, Waldron, Riccardi—
developed what was always the most hearty

bond connecting us till we finished high
school and prepared us to reach for the sky

as we went our own ways to study law,
the Bible or medicine. We looked and saw

what would make us special. And Mike did nudge
his experience thus to be a judge

of the Superior Court in LA
without regard to stature or to pay.

Mike fit to justice like a hand in glove
And he did it with a heart full of love.

Where Has Love Gone?

I will not allow the masquerade
of our cordial handshake to dissolve
the reality of who we have been.

Our coupled palms remind me of your hand's magic.
That hand softly and sweetly caressed my cheek.
That hand guided me into your essence.

That hand made the volcano erupt,
white lava adorning your hair and puddling
in the voluptuous crevice of your breasts.

I miss your touch and wonder where has love gone?

Will

I broke my neck once—
in a Massachusetts lake.
For some two and one-half minutes,
facedown, motionless in the water,
I pondered free will.

Every cell of me demanded
that I inhale deeply, gasp.
Who I am, what I am, what I was
said No! I did not, would not gasp.

Rescued, mouth exposed to air, I relented.
I gasped, then whispered: "I'm dying.
I've broken my neck."

Part of me did die that day.
But, I did not.
I willed.

Wine Day in Absentia

To savor wine
that only samples
is but to taste in part;
and give presence to
what might be tasted.

The indelible presence of
that simply sampled wine
lingers and at times
intrudes on that full-tasted.

Printed in the United States
by Baker & Taylor Publisher Services